LAMENT IN A MINOR KEY

A selection of poems

Maire Liberace

LAMENT IN A MINOR KEY

A selection of poems
by Maire Liberace

Clachan Publishing
3 Drumavoley Park, Ballycastle, BT54 6PE,
Glens of Antrim, Northern Ireland.

Email: info@clachanpublishing.com
Website: http://clachanpublishing-com.

ISBN : 978-1-909906-45-7

Published 2018

TABLE OF CONTENTS

ACKNOWLEDGEMENTS

This collection of poems was inspired by many people and events, and I was encouraged along the process of creation by many supporters and mentors. First and foremost, my good friend and colleague, Dan Masterson, Poet Laureate of Rockland County, who has for many years guided and encouraged my efforts, and also served as an inspiration, reader and gentle critic. To my very good friend and colleague, Wilma Frank, we have laughed and cried together, and celebrated life. Fr. Joe Kelly who has always been a mentor for me as I journey through the years of my life and shared in the birthing of my ideas, vision and hopes.

I especially thank my family, Mairead, my computer guru, award winning Art Director and Designer. She generously created the cover illustration. Ellen, Rose, James and Sonya, who shared love, laughter, good food and wine. A special thanks to Robert, for contributing his artistic genius again with the internal illustrations, and to Lina, Celia and Ava for their love and support. They all have tolerated my activities with humor, love and laughter in the middle and muddle of their own busy lives. Bob, you encouraged and pushed me to grow, shared your passion for music and art and enriched my life.

I cannot omit my Irish family in Ballycastle and environs, I thank you all for your love, welcome always and being my family. I am so lucky!

To my many friends here in New York, thank you for your friendship, it is a glorious gift.

A big 'Thank you' to Sean O'Halloran and Clachan Publishing for your efforts in bringing my work to life. Your wise input and suggestions make the process

ABOUT THE AUTHOR

Maire Keena Liberace was born in Dublin, Ireland and she renews her Irish sensibility each summer in Ballycastle, a place dear to her. She currently lives in New York where she is a Professor of Philosophy and Speech at SUNY Rockland Community College. She has a Distinguished Service Professorship from the (State University of New York) SUNY Board of Trustees and is a member of the SUNY Distinguished Academy. She has published poetry in several texts and anthologies and has written procedural manuals for business and industry. She is the author of Walking on Water, poems celebrating her childhood memories in Ireland. She is also the author of "The Ethics of Organizations: A Mandate for Management" and the editor of "The Life, Career, and Educational Planning " textbook.

ABOUT THE ILLUSTRATOR

Robert Liberace is known for his classic and distinctive style of drawing, painting and sculpture. He was selected as a "Living Master" by the Art Renewal Center, is an honorary member of the American China Oil Painting Artist League and is a selected member of the National Sculpture Society. His work has been highlighted in a variety of publications. He was the recipient of the Portrait Society's Grand Prize award in their International Competition. He teaches at the Art League of Virginia, the Portrait Society's annual conferences, and holds workshops throughout the United States and abroad.

THESE POEMS ARE DEDICATED TO
MY FATHER,

DR. JAMES P. KEENA, FRCP&SI

A MAN FAMILIAR WITH THE
DISSONANCE AND DISRUPTION OF LIVES
ASSOCIATED WITH INTERNMENT, AND
TO ALL THOSE WHOSE LIVES WERE
DISRUPTED BY A PROCESS MORE OFTEN
ENGENDERED BY SUSPICION
AND HATE.

By the rivers of Babylon
We sat and wept
As we remembered Zion
Psalm 137

Courtesy of Robert Liberace

EXECUTIVE ORDER 90   66

(...immediate evacuation of all persons of Japanese lineage, and all others, aliens and citizens alike, whose presence shall be deemed dangerous or inimical to the defense of the United States.
Recommendations, Assistant Secretary U.S. War Record 107)

I

At four I could see my face
reflected in the sheets of water
that seemed a permanent fixture on the landscape,
mine looked like all the other faces
that moved around my day,
my mother, father, grandfather,
my baby sister, the only bud blooming
in the infertile soil.

My father, one of the Issei,
said I owned the land around
because I was a Nisei
and that my children would be Sansei,
but I need to mention nothing
of these things to others.

and so I learned to keep silent
even as I watched the white neighbors
with their big eyes move away,
even as more who looked like me
moved into the vacant houses
began to till the land
plant chrysanthemums and tomatoes.

II

The year was 1942, I was eight on February 27.
I could taste the air blowing in
from the Pacific, a salty acrid taste
that gnawed like little teeth,
my mother hid my flashlight
because last night she found me
throwing lighted circles on the ceiling
while she waited for my father to come home,
she was afraid because she said the authorities
dug up the garden patch next door,
the tomatoes in their lot pointed
to the airfield, so the soldiers said.
I could not imagine planes landing
on the small strip of grass
running along the sidewalk and wondered
what I would do if a pilot knocked
at the door looking for directions,
where would I send him?

III

Late that night my father came into my room
and said that we had seven days to sell our house
we had to gather all that we could carry
some bedding, toilet articles, cutlery
no pets, no, not my canary, no mattresses,
we were to be guests of the U.S. army
going to a place called Heart Mountain, Wyoming,
there, see it on the map, way up north of here.

And so in the early morning hours two days later,
bags and rolls of bedding and the few small
suitcases borrowed from some kind people
all tagged and tied together we bussed
from Berkley past the Bay Bridge
across town to Tanforan race track.
my father said this was the assembly center
where we would board the train.
Delight at seeing horses was quickly quashed

by the sight of barbed wire fences, watch towers,
armed guards, sentries at the gates posted
with their guns at ready, to protect us
my mother whispered. But I could never understand
why those guns pointed right at me.
they hustled us off the bus, moved us toward
the grandstand, dumped our baggage on the growing
heap inside the gate. Numbers were handed out,
3536798 instead of our name, "use only that for
identification", a stable number, a horse stall number,
a letter for the space where we could move around.

and then we got two army blankets,
a bag to fill with straw piled at the grandstand,
this would be our mattress, then quick march
to our horse stall just as the wind picked up
carrying in mists of rain from the bay.
any vestige of grass was now a sea of mud
which sloshed over our shoes, seeped
into our socks and spattered everything we had
before we reached the crude hut, our shelter.

the stall was cold and damp and smelly
dust had spread a fine layer on the floor
the walls were greyed with cobwebs laced
with hay and dead insects
the only thing we had to clean was
the whisk broom my mother smuggled in
tucked under her skirt as if she had a wish
to brush these events out of existence.
our few meager belongings we used
to stop cracks in the wooden boards

the chill breezes still whistled through
pulling at our clothes as we huddled together
listening to the sobs and crying drifting over
the stall dividers, a lament in a minor key
competing with the whistle of wind and thrum

4

of rain on the galvanized roof, the bass rumble
of snoring, the high sibilance of whispers,
all this disharmony drifts in and out my dreams
the rest of my sleeping life.

Curfew call became the boundaries of our days
the litany of names broken by new arrivals
or the departure of bodies in a rickety hearse.
police patrolled, mail was inspected,
sheet and blankets became the walls of privacy,
we slept, ate, snored, dressed and undressed
in one continuous public performance
always waiting, waiting, for the washroom,
for food, for medicals, to go home.

IV

In March we pack and move again,
escorted to the station, names and numbers
checked against a list, luggage inspected
we were bundled on the train,
so many people, so little space and
I could not see my friends.

Tucked into a window corner
I noticed someone had nailed it shut,
I used my sleeve to scrub the grimy pane
squinted into the morning greyness
for some familiar landmark to anchor me
until a guard told me to draw the shades,
"they were to be drawn from dawn to dusk".
my mother was long lost in silence
even my father looked smaller
shrunken into the crowd of people
and baggage that filled our carriage.
As the train rattled and creaked through
the days and nights (I counted four)
children cried, parents sat stiff and weary-eyed,
I wandered the passages between compartments
dodged the guards who paced up and down

and tried to figure just where
it was that we were going.
I brought water and fruit to my parents
who seemed to have forgotten English
assured them of my safety and behavior
so they would have no cause to worry.

V

Heart Mountain!
the train stopped,
my body rocked, still in rhythm
with the silenced clack of wheels on tracks
doors were pulled open
flushing the stale air
weak light flooded the carriage
highlighting tired and drawn faces
the soldiers hustled the crowd
out onto the platform
a concrete island in a desert
empty of trees, shrubs, grass,
in the distance a lone mountain
broke the horizon.

Heart Mountain,
godforsaken place
where the wind blew a ceaseless whirl of dust,
the soil, a gummy mess in winter,
turned into hard baked ridges in the heat of summer
trees brought in to create beauty and shelter
died before they bloomed
stifled by the harsh climate.
"do they cut out our hearts and bury them here?"
they did for some, my mother said
then narrowed her eyes
and said that mine would be next
if I did not do the family honor.

6

Stretching into the far horizon
row upon row of low buildings
covered with tar-paper etched parallel lines,
again the soldiers, fences, barbed wire,
watch towers, bare beams and rafters,
army cots, rationed food, bells for meals,
we grouped together in the dining hall
at our designated times, gulped our food,
just another crowded, noisy event.

Our summers choked with dust and sweat
winter wrapped the place in bitter cold
each evening I filled our chipped enamel pails
with water and woke in the grey
dawn to find them covered
with a thin skim of ice
my clothes, too light to keep me warm,
I stuffed with rags and paper
I had no gloves but found that
paper bags worked well
except when they got wet,
a depression in a hollow filled with water
became a skating rink and then a pool
in summer, until some boys got sick,
the wind and mud and snow
robbed my dreams, I longed for home.

Assigned one room per family
at night I helped my father
search for discarded government lumber,
we made tables, chairs, room dividers,
my mother labored to plant flowers and vegetables,
skinny strips of green poked out the soil
as the weak rays of winter warmed to spring
but shriveled in the blasts of hot air
and shrunk into the midsummer dust
she gave up, grew smaller, quieter,
spent hours staring at the looming mountain
or in bed if no one was around.

VI

The men formed work details
sharing hammers, scavenged nails, saws,
shovels, lengths of rope.
they built long splintery benches
put them in an unused shack
where they set up a school, started classes,
corralled those who could to teach,
anything to keep us busy and alive.
my mother, put in charge of organizing
class times, students, teachers,
suddenly came alive and roped me in
to run errands, write lists, lick envelopes,
watch my baby sister, anything to occupy my time
and keep me "out of trouble".

Late at night young men held meetings, talked loud,
dropped to whispers at each sound outside,
bitterness and cynicism poured poison
into their gatherings as they faced
the constant threat of government edicts
and decisions where they had no input,
meetings were held in latrines and boiler rooms
I sneaked around listening through chinks
in the wood, tried to make meaning out
of the muffled voices as they rose and fell
like the cadence of the sea I missed so much,
but then the meetings stopped
their daily paper was shut down
they moved the leaders
to some other places far away
my mother kept my father busy
so he would not join those troublemakers
I had to stay at home.

Our lives began to develop a routine
that followed the one we had when we were free
chores, school, play, homework,

8

we had a baseball league
and learned to sled with dustbin lids in winter
there were big parties for new babies, weddings,
everyone helped when grandfather became sick and died,
and every mother watched to see that every child
was doing what they were supposed to do.

Days blurred into each other
seasons were measured by the things we did not do,
no Christmas trees, no fireworks in July,
no trips to other places, no friends to stay,
the year was a repeated wallpaper pattern
flowing from room to room,
listening to the whispered conversations
or loud laughter of the guards
as they talked about the yellow peril
even as my parents and their friends
talked and schemed about returning to Japan
a place I did not want to know,
I longed to see my Japanese face disappear.

VII

November 1945, a magic date and word
Relocation!
excitement stirred the camp
and started talk and dreams of home,
yet the stories coming in said our homes were gone
our land was sold, others had moved in,
so where was home?
They released us
photographed and fingerprinted,
we climbed aboard the train,
the doors slammed, a whistle blew,
the train jerked back then forward,
chuffed out of the station
and slowly picked up speed.
forty two blocks of tar-paper barracks
vanished into the night.

Courtesy of Robert Liberace

10

A fire that consumes
Psalm 18

Courtesy of Robert Liberace

13

PRISMS

I would fly this place
if I could find scissor
sharp enough to sever
woven bonds that enmesh
my limbs in strident rooms

wings beat on dusty panes
until their thrusts
echo in my mind
scattering thoughts
in whirls of autumn
winds showering skyward
brown and gold confetti

fountains in a courtyard
weep tears hued with
crystal colors gathered
into dusky pools
mirroring in their depths
the star pocked skies

rain moistens dust
inscribing circles
on the surface
of the stillness
then sinks and merges
into rainbow waters
reflecting bronze
beacons radiating
from street lamps

in the darkened room
a voice sings the barren
walls to dazzling luminescence
and loosens cords
that bind my soul
ascending to the light
in one pure perfect note.

COCOON

Twenty nine years
she walked in the shadow
of his might
a background of beige and browns
demure as a neat cornered
lace edged handkerchief
apeep from a hidden pocket

every morning
at seven precise
she warmed his Times to crisp
later
ankles crossed hands tight folded
nodded in vigorous agreement
with his every
boomed pronouncement
on the state of the universe

in the secret afternoon
she perused with quiet anticipation
the daily horoscopes
hers Gemini, his Cancer,
unaware
of the unseen crab
eroding the inflexible bond
a silent invader
stealing through
the tight webbed tunnels
severing inexorably
the links in the silver chain

until there remained
an empty shell
scooped out transparent
discarded

on the barren beach of her life
a cold bed still dented
with the shape
that no longer broke her night
with prolonged shufflings
and shiftings

now the house echoes
with the hollow emptiness
of a tomb
leaving her filled
with the sour heartburn
of resentment.

TOO LONG A SACRIFICE

I sit on the parched grass
at the bottom of the meadow
my back absorbing the rough
caress of the yew

the dying rays of the sun
bleed over the horizon
behind me the house
looms a shadow

as I wait for the night
a magician
with disappearing boxes
hidden under dark cloths

in the blaze of the afternoon
your burning body invaded the stagnant heat
I felt your hands search my every cavity
your thick breath
burrowed into my ear
curled in whorls around my head
my membranes cringed taut and dry
my body slaked under your weight

while I unsheathed
the thin sharp blade
of anger honed
by your brutal thrusts
scraping the skin off
years shrouded in silence

watching it bleed
silently sinking
into the rumpled sheets
the sagging mattress…
this handful of dry dirt
crumbles through my fingers
the night grows cold.

THE FIRST STAGE: DENIAL

She turns her back on voices
voices do not know the truth,
they crescendo, waver, diminish
buzzing like mosquitoes
she sees his body curled
as he always sleeps
head angled to the edge
of the rumpled pillow

she hears the hammering in her ears
which thump an echo in his hollowed chest
her hand grasps his
feels its slack coldness
knows her warmth
will stir response
but he always sleeps
so deep in dreams

she bends her head
presses her lips on his
Wonders at the tinge of blue
Sure that she can stir
the icy lines to pink tumescence
and wake him to the dawn
angling sunlight through
the half drawn shades.

THE SECOND STAGE

The pine logs lay where he had worked them
just before the buzz-saw whined its quicksilver
through bone a clean cut exposing nerves, muscles,
sinews,
before the flapping edge retracted pulsing a flood
splashing down his shirt oozing over his trousers
and spreading a dark stain on the cement floor
heaped with sawdust which cushioned his fall.

The moon had turned a cycle
when she crossed again from house to barn
the latch on the hand-hewn door was stiff
the rusty hinges moaned in protest
as she dragged it shut turning slowly
to the darkness the lantern held high
threw a small glow, kind in its dimness,
it shadow- peopled the rough oak beams and corners
stacked with bins and bales of straw

hooking its handle on a rusted nail
angling up from the center support strut
she wrenched the axe out of the scarred
ash stump once a shelter over the front porch
now a catchall for pliars, wrenches, hammers,
she felt the smooth sheen of the shaft
polished by his hands weathered as his lean body
the thin line of the blade tip still oiled
and honed to a sharp sliver

tightening her grip, hefting its weight
she heaved it back and slammed it down
hacking at the machine until its springs
nuts and bolts
spilled out and mingled
with her burning tears, the mounds of sawdust
and the rusty stains etched into the cement.

MORPHOSIS

A glass of wine toasted nightly
to an empty chair
did not assuage the hollow chill
that swelled the day
and crept into the night
a windowless room waiting
for another gray dawn.

shuffling automatic through
the pointless chores
life condensed to one room
one cup one plate

and then…
Spring came
pushing tentative fingers
through the cracks
splintering the brittle ice
into muddied pools

an early blossom plucked
in a moment of abandon
laid against her withered cheek
faint perfume wafted
like a silken scarf
in concentric circles
a cathedral rose window
radiating showers of
peacock pinks
delphinium blues
kingfisher darts of color
pulsing out the attic
of her memory

moving her to turn
the new moist earth
digging deep to bed the seed

that in June would yield
to scarlet pokers overhung
with blowsy red roses
dripping their seductive
fragrance into the heavy night.

THE COLOR OF LONELINESS

slate sea
reflects
gray sky
gulls
mewl
dissonant
wind
wails
around
the barn
empty
windows
dark
night
animals
howl and bay
sounds that
tear into
the soul.

WIRED

I remake myself
tumble down the bones
string muscles on a line
to blow dry,
wintery gasps
whistle
through bare hedges
grey cells
clump
beside red pools
quiver
merge and mound
into plasmic globes
glo-in-the-dark
radonic waves
pulse out
catch the eyeball's gleam
lash fringed they flicker
spark and sizzle
watch words
tumble together
to create
a new world song
it hums along
the wires
entwines
the disjointed parts
in electric vibratos.

A BREAK IN THE STORM

Light spirals down
shafts of silver
strike solid rock
and splinter out
in fiery sparks

as the blacksmith
strikes the hot iron
raising the hammer
muscles bulge and strain
he slams it down
on the red hot glow
pincered on the anvil.

For everything there is a season
Ecclesiastes ch. 3

Courtesy of Robert Liberace

AUTUMN ADVENT

First a dropping
A small scattering
of still green leaves
shaken by the turning winds
then a ripening
a bursting into fullness
like a pregnant woman
reaching her ninth month
autumn creeps in over
the brown grass of August
the moon, sated by heat,
hangs rich and low
blushing in her wantonness
she wraps herself
in morning mists
nature with abandon
paints the horizon
dipping her brush
into random colors
which splash and spill
on shrubs, trees and flowers.

EARLY FALL '85

Slow moving to the early dark
bright-blaze red lit
flaming the holding air
last days of hovering heat
lazing days
and yet containing movement
to a tightening
turning of the jade
the moss, the emerald
to brilliants,
yellows, gold, flashing crimsons
dropping off and brown carpeting
crisp rustled underfoot
all visible, to be caught
swirled high aloft
by mighty breaths
heralding the advent
of icy fingers
which touch all
holding in entombed silence
life,
that with the lengthening days
will stretch out and up
to soft spreading warmth.

LATE AUTUMN

Cold winds, a touch of frost
have stripped your finery
an ageing whore all that remains
of your seductive glory are
pouting parasitic berries
overripe scarlet splashing
the barren air with brazen promise
a trailing scarf still golden hued
clings to de-fleshed limbs and
bony prominences black with age
tatters of a fruitful summer
scattered round your bare-rooted feet
blend with the deep moss plush velvet
slippering the vacant spaces,
the fallen apples, speckled with
brown blight from early spring,
mush into slurry fermenting the air
you can no longer bend to wintery gusts
but creak and moan still clinging
to the rich brown loam that
bore and nurtured your first
delicate unravished innocence
awaiting with defiance your
last caller from the North Country.

WINTER SUNSET

Etched sharp by frigid air
the evening burns a vivid orange
along the far horizon
blazing a light-glow into the domed
night-blue sky
the penitential trees stretch heavenward
tall and silent
topmost branches ruffing out in lacy
silhouettes
winter's advent freezes all in still-frame
clarity
somewhere a night-maiden slowly tamps
the bright
cupping her hands around the incandescent
daystar
she draws a blue-black velvet cover over
all the earth.

CAMEO IN DECEMBER

My steps crisp crunch
across the pristine surface
to the log pile
huddled near the back porch
hunched into scarf and coat
I feel the cold attack
drawing tears
pinching my face
pulling my fingers
into balled fists

the smell of fires
rising to the skies
singes the night air
and the stars
Drop down their sparkle
to hang on evergreens
and shrubs flames
of blue and orange
green and white

under the weight of snow
shellacked with crystal
trees crack and creak
ice hardened to the core
like old bones
scrape and rub
one on the other
shooting their barbs
into every movement

one deep drawn breath
sears my lungs
exhaled air hangs
in puffy clouds
around my head as
I retrace my path

placing my feet into
the jagged indentations
careful not to drop
my rough barked burden.

WINTERING OUT

I turn
the light
to sun
the cold
and
brighten corners

where
ice
gathers
in long
fingers

layering
clothes
hibernating
into
steamy
warmth

seeing
the cat's
sleekness
fluff into
ginger
clouds

I hug her heat
To the cold sheets
And listen
To the wind
Howling
In the bare branches.

ISOTACHS

The black mountains
are patched with April snow
here under the lee of the house
the forsythia spark yellow florets,
purple crocuses shrug off last night's
ermine mantle
lift their heads to the sun,
nod to the awakening daffodils,

the sudden sharp light unveils
the winter debris
shards of glass, discarded cans,
bottle caps, scraps of paper,
flags of plastic trapped
on low brambles,

in the heart the stir
to change quickens the blood
shoots laser beams to
torpid muscles
tingles the fingers
propels the body into action
like points of equal wind speeds.

REBIRTH

The ice sheath drawn over
the rounded earth
conceals the silent turning
moments of warmth sparkle
across the crystalline surface
give new color to
the slender willow fronds
dance past the tight folded
buds peeking on the magnolia

earth sleeps light
in the early morning
holding still
in the chill
preceding sunrise
pushed back to dormancy
by clouds sprinkling
large soft flakes
blown by ice edged breaths
still streaming from the north

tentatively
out of the elemental womb,
unnoticed under the detritus
last remnants of fall,
tips push upward
white blooms green stippled
in the land there is
a hint of fragrance wafted
by an errant southern breeze
days lengthen
and the wintered birds
stir with shrill aggression

tingling then letting down
the breasts of earth release
the flow nourishing

hidden roots, rising sap
running in rivulets,
the earth sups
with passionate abandon.

PROMISES OF SPRING

Gray day
and the leafless
branches out my window
drip moisture

the crisp winter
has been muffled
by February fog

your gift brings spring
early to my year
a pot of crocus garbed
in Lenten purple

hands folded tight behind
a grill of narrow leaves
tulips in full bloom
their gay peach and gold

a sun on my desk
primulas lemon yellow
a hint of orange
grouped like a gaggle

of giggling schoolchildren,
open faced these nosegays
burst into my drab day

blooming like fireworks
on a july night
then fizzling into
curling grey smoke.

My soul shall weep in secret
places
Jeremiah 13

Courtesy of Robert Liberace

DEATH IN SUBURBIA

LOT 6, PLOT L, TOWN - PLANNING MAP

Three days ago they invaded
the wilderness rampant
across the street

the crayola yellow
machines belching
non-stop noise
cut swathes of ugly
through the shuddering
trees davening
and bending
in prayers pleading

their maws chewed wads
of dirt spewing them
to the sides,
clodded graves
baked by the sun
to hard linear sculptures

on the third day
the lot was empty
with the still of Sabbath

the trees were buried
the weeping woman
rolled her door shut
against the nakedness.

BETTER TO LIGHT A CANDLE THAN CURSE THE DARK

Hot white
a blade of light
shafts upward
from the straight

virginal body
not yet distorted
by spent life
drops
melted heat

spilling over
to the base
it clumps
in rounded heaps

smoke grimed
shadowed and unlit.

The flame sputters
sparks and disappears.

SEARCH FOR MEANING

I search for words
thumb through Roget
flick from page to page
weigh the meaning etched
in black and white
but

words
are nurtured
in the sun
allowed
to form and change
as new sprung grass
to play
together in the vast space
of a mountain meadow
picked
like daisies
and woven into
circlets
of white and gold
adorning dreams
strung together
like colored beads
on an abacus
they slip
through pursed lips
like clotted cream
break
like crisp biscuits
melt velvet on the tongue
soulspeak
they lightly skip
over meandering paths
trace
songlines tell histories

in the firelight
conjure
summer langour autumn crackle
or winter's icy prisms
sensate
as fur on the underbelly
of a kitten
they touch
springs that leap
from mind to mind.

STICKS AND STONES

Fractured light
splinters from
the chandelier
multicolored
motes swirling
in the crack
of voices rising,
an angry ferment
scouring the
polished parquet
notched with years
of abuse

somewhere
in the silence
left by the closing
of the door
a clock ticks

the circling hands
sweeping away
the minutes of
breath-held
silence
that sharpen
the moment

a razor-edged sword
cutting the air
the final words
hang suspended
in the vacant space

echo and re-echo
through the hollowed
mind until they drop
like stones

into a deep well
sliding silkily
through still waters

touching bottom
in elemental
slime.

THE NIGHT HAS A THOUSAND EYES

Implacable the moon stares into the dark pool
watching the night
her face reflects
the slow turning from black to grey
to luminous pearl,
brushing against the rocky edges of the shore
the waters stir and murmur
small gossips, hidden melodies,
in the murky depths
the drowned town holds secrets
shared only with the fish
as they swim in and out the gaping windows,
the remaining doors swing to and fro
moved by hidden currents that swirl along the bottom
lifting puffs of silt, forgotten debris
spilled out of abandoned attics and basements

shadow pines stretch back from the shores
they catch the secret whispers of hidden life
waft them through the needles like gentle breezes,
voices from the past calling home the cows
or clucking to chickens hiding in roosts
deep in the cool dark of the forest,
in a clearing a circle of tombstones
fix the time and place in history
and spell out names to the stars
in the mournful hoot of owls nested
in ivy thickly tangled over flattened mounds,
the echoes float over the water
and blend with the call of loons
circling their young on the surface of the still water.

TRANSPLANT

There is a need to live where lanes
are dark
and bushes tangle with each other
hiding in their hearts the music of
the hours
where you can hear the murmuring
of night
or songs from peepers in a hidden
swamp
each new day dawning
the sun will stretch his arms
above the misty light
and drink the grasses dry
of dew that blessed them
in the cool of night

and oak and ash will embrace
the house with shade
that dances on the windowsill
a feeding ledge for cardinals
bright in red
with tufted caps upon their heads
unmoved by raucous cries
of jays blue bright
against the azure sky

this is the dream that fills the day
as traffic snarls and growls
on dusty streets
and as the day slips into dark
unblinking eyes glare down on
rain slicked pavements
inscribing burnished gold rectangles
reflecting a hellish blush onto the
black above and filling
the room and soul
with angry light.

VALLEY FORGE

Scudding clouds play tag around the moon
shadows flit over the fields
slip in around the trees
in the underbrush sounds of furtive
footsteps rustle fall crisped leaves
snap fallen twigs and branches
with gun sharp retorts
in the puffs of wind
a breath caught,
in surprise or panic,
ripples grasses
Ethereals move about
the land, drift into the wind

in this field the alarm of battle
the hurry of preparations
wrapped in stealthy movements
is caught in the mists that hang
over the low valleys
and swirl around the bluffs
where ghosts stumble around
disoriented by steel
highways ad roaring traffic.

VETERANS CEMETRY

Standing silhouetted against the soft evening sky
his shadow measures the length of the flat green
touching toes with the silence

the stillness mirrored
in the square pillow
of concrete
that marks
the bed

at ease
hands clasped behind
he does not break
at the sharp crack
of the pennant
whipping in the brisk breeze

his memory holds no terror
of sudden sounds
unseen enemies

yet he is linked with the mud tossed relic
that survives beyond body mutilated
laid to rest

arcing forward he traces
the lettering with a finger
delicate with resurrection
recreating a face
a voice
an image
to fill the void
of this february day
hunched
against the growing chill
he wraps his arms around his body
shivering
with the still empty loss.

4 A.M., THE RUSTED ANCHOR, BOSTON HARBOR

About damaged men who shrink into the quiet
at the mercy of a madwoman whose kiss
made them drunk with love fermenting a riot
in the cells that took a miss-measure of the abyss
where they lay stabbed by the branches of dead trees
trees that will not sprout green shade in a june
summer or host tangled vines of sweet peas
butterflying on the lower trunks before they prune
the leggy stems and case them in crystal
vases which shoot electric sparks above the bar
where scant clad girls belly up and hold a pistol
grip on glasses filled with amber and listen to a guitar
plucked notes twanging dissonance while they brood
on love among the disillusioned
and how it will conclude.

RUINED CHOIRS

Near a copse of barren trees
stripped of green
where no birds sing
a circling of ravens
sweeps the empty sky
narrow and narrower
the black spiral
funnels down
tightens
wings batter the air
the rhythm ululates
with echoing vibrations.

Sodden mist
shifts in drifts
over rocked walls,
the dilapidated ruin..
a sudden noise, a falling branch
or distant thunder
disrupts the gyration

the group reverses
fans out in disarray
swirls
to the nearest treetop
where they perch
black leaves
on bare branches.

STEALING FORTY

The sun peaked to high noon intensity
glares klieg light through the window
I close my eyes softly drawing
finger pads across the concealed orbs
circumscribing bony promontories…

pansies fresh with dark-eyed innocence
fringe the edge of conscious thought
dissolving into sensuous velvet
flashing lights of golden yellow
bloom around the jagged border
marigolded into summer sun
blinding the softer spring,
thoughts, scattered fragments,
dart like meteorites
leaving trails of silvery light
clinging
in the way of spider threads
spun at dawn, unraveled
in the brighter noon…

REACH OUT AND TOUCH SOMEONE

Pushing the buttons
I listen
to the beeps
leaping
the miles

hoping
to jar
your ears
with measured
chords

the click
of lifting
and I know
the air
is not empty

I measure
your day
by tone
of voice
and weight
of word.

STONE MASON AT WORK

Digging the trench
leveling the bottom
with flinted stones
he starts the project
aligning the path
with fragile string
stake anchored
at random intervals

the rocks garnered
over seasons of planting
lie to the side
in ungainly barren piles
slowly, painstakingly
he moves the mountain
stopping now and then
to study line and angle

resting on the narrow hilt
he tucks his foot firmly
against the wooden shaft
of the spade relaxing
his grip on the handle
swiping his arm across
his forehead his shirt
absorbs the gritty tears
of sweat streaking
his cheeks

he surveys his handiwork
with a seasoned eye
feeling in his muscles
the weight and heft
of every rock

spitting on his palms
rubbing them together
he bends to the work again
numb to the pain of torn skin
crushed knuckles blood caked,

boulders rolled
pushed
jacked
one atop the other
blending greys, browns, slate
a touch of shining quartz
the wall grows and shapes
it girds around
not yet high enough
to keep the world at bay
not yet secure enough
to contain the secrets
of the inner house
but now defines by its circling
the limits
of entrances and exits,

maybe planted with aubretia
aspects of stone will soften
into golden color
waterfalling down to green.

SANDCASTLE DREAMS

The smell of low tide hung in the afternoon
scuffing aimlessly with his feet and hands
he crouched on the summer sand
building a castle maybe a dream
above the waterline

but the grains fell in silky rivers
not holding sharp corners of angled turns
and so he moved the sculpting
to where the sand was packed
and firmed by morning's high tide

his work now strained with purpose
carving and curving the lines
mountains, valleys,
seeing a figure evolve

fingers shape the outline of a leg
thumbs smooth the roundness
of thighs rising to a fullness

of buttock where his hands paused
to feel the contours against palms
sensing the silkiness of flesh,
the smell of desire tingling
his fingertips
along the slender line of back

blending into one arm flung overhead
revealing an arc of breast glinting
in the fading rays of sun
touched a tenderness springing
tears that stung his eyes

his work could make a dream unfold
create an Eve to people empty shores

lovers coupling under cormorants
whirling in shrill criticism

with seaweed tendrils
he framed
the neck and hid the unformed face
he did not feel the greedy waves
lick enviously around his feet

creep over his naked heat
and with a rapine surge
scoop away
the creation of the afternoon.

DEFENSE

My words rise up
flutter like ribbons
in a summer breeze
or jet streams
from silvered planes
high beyond visible

sometimes they dance and rustle
green fans cooling the heat,
or browned by hot winds
drop

crisp and sharp
littering the ground
where they are crushed
by heedless feet
or swept away
into the gutter
by a sudden downpour.

BUTTERFLY

Remembering nights of music and silk dresses
she watched a moth beat its wings
against the window screen
desperate to reach the light
that sliced a wedge of amber
across the narrow room

beyond the window in the looming dark
clouds clumped together oppressed the sky
light bolts from dark to dark
like thoughts, sparking from caverns
deep in the mind's recesses,
surge up as birds at a certain season
feeling the warm air under their wings
take flight into the blue vastness

despite the powders and the creams
the years crowded in with
scars and calloused skin
gay flashing scarves and bright colors
did little to disguise the woman
lying in the valley of the bed
who did not want to spend the night alone.

RECLUSE

Sap-dried and soured of hope
she sits in her cluttered den
among the discarded copies
of the daily papers
yellowing in the light
that struggles
through the windows
grimed with dust and dirt

the television flickering
through the dim
reflects an alien world
cobwebs dip and hammock
in the corners hooking
to books, baubles, bric-a-brac

smoke hazes around her
from cigarettes lit
and stubbed
one after one
until the ashtray
brims over
onto the small table
watermarked with linking circles.

Daring, children scrabble
through the privet hedge
gaped from trespassers,
crawl through the towering
grass and weeds,
the debris scattered
under the shadowing elms
the tottering house

they climb on the stone ledges
cushioned with verdigris
and press their faces
up against the panes
their flattened noses
and puckered lips
swim like fish
past her dulled eyes,

the muffled laughter
swivels her head
and for an instant
she is skipping
on a sunlit street.

RETROSPECTIVE: BRIDGE STREET, MOUNTMELLICK

Stone bridges granite banked water
brown floods spill over concreted feet
visible on days where daggered light
stabbed through green scum
surface floating points
picked through swaying algae
cans, bottles, flotsam,
jetsam jettisoned from
the parapets, schoolboys perfecting
their aim, as they streeled home
in late afternoons
loosened from wooden desks,
crumpled paper, chalk dusted windows,
drone induced dreams
of distant playing fields
waves of people and the crack
of ash on leather

ink stained, their fingers slipped
under water ice cold, reached
for minnows, turned rocks,
darted back from startled crayfish,
socks, shoes discarded they waded
into the forbidden depths,
behind their backs
the church steeple glowered
their omissions and commissions
shadowed the stony ground around
the convent where windows squinted,
noted the faces and marked
an invisible roster.

NIGHT WATCH

Winter cuts short the light
evening lengthens through the windows
shadow-shrouding the room

the last glimmer fades from the sky
into a bleak emptiness

she peers through the gloom
at the night shapes

marking with faint surprise
their changing into the
fringed edge of her nightmares

in the far distance the low hum
alerts her body to rigid quiet

holding her breath taut
her ears tense into deafness
with a quickening pulse

through the dark twin eyes
play hide
-and-seek in and out
the trees until they suddenly

loom close
floodlighting the dark lawn
the frozen silhouette of her waiting

and pass on
she slumps relaxing the knotted muscles

her hands still clenched knuckle white
around the support ledge
under the darkened window.

MOONBALM

Last night I saw the moon
suspended from an invisible thread
a silver sliver in a not dark sky
I wondered if I could climb so high,
imagined the hand-over-hand effort,
the violent sway back and forth
high over the darkened earth
twinkling with a myriad lights
reflected from homing cars,
crowded stores, crisscrossed highways,
cramped cities, nestled suburbs,
and, here and there, on the mountain
a lone house, its light
a small freckle in the night,
I could almost breathe the clean air
could feel the rush of high winds
as I stepped down into the inner curve
and nested in the milky glow.

NEAPOLITAN MUSE

Parthenope plays memory like a lyre
Fingering the bones
Strumming the notes that sing the body,
Its height, the play of muscles,
The stretch of tendons.

Thrusting towards land
he swims under the shadow
of Vesuvius' dark breasts
veined with milky streams,
the glittering fall of water,
a crystal cascade,
slicks the skin
drawn taut in effort,
the sun floods his laughing mouth
as the music mingles with the waves.

Watching from her perch
astride the brined rocks
she draws him closer,
her obsidian eyes the magnets
that lure men to their death
as her sea-wracked hair
swirls hypnotically
in the ebb and flow of grey-blue waters.

Shadows painted by the sun
filter through now hollowed eyes,
fill the cranial cave,
the dark passages echo
with a melody surfacing through half-sleep
open mouth and bared teeth
mock restringing the dream.

MEN DANCE ON DEATHLESS FEET

Men dance on deathless feet
pressing the sprung grass
their songs hum winds
in patterned circles
budding the bare air
starlight pierces dark
to sun-hammered gold
dusted on the flying hair
the touching fingers
I see the earth with clear eyes.

The music dances deep into the night
God breathing in the dark
strums wind to rustle green waves
through the tall trees
the forest ocean dashes
on a branchy shore
first rain flicks
pebble showers
on window panes
filling the air
with the musky smell
of new washed earth.

HOSTILE ACTS

Clouds, black edged with purple,
dark hands covering the sun,
roll in from the western horizon
the air oppressive,
boding in its stillness,
mutes the birds as they retreat
to hide among the stilled leaves

this sullen silence is broken
by an occasional blast of air
ruffling the tree tops
a thief riffling through bits and pieces
for hidden baubles then

discards the fake with lightening speed
as his hot breath sullies
the room leaving an imprint of evil
that lurks long past his flight

the inchoate howls
locked behind the rigid cage
of bone and muscle struggle
to burst out and blend
with the storm that circles
in ever narrowing orbits
like a beast approaches
its prey mesmerizing
the cowering animal
struck motionless.

FIRE STARTER

Raking the embers of the heart
bares from the ashes
scorched remnants
of what was a life
threaded with ribbons
streaming in soft-spoken
southern winds
rippling rainbows of blue
aqua, red rose,
violet, yellow,
yellow as the early spring
when hope bloomed bright
forsythia sprays

winter moved the sun
a different angle
fertile earth becomes
a brown and barren desert
hosts hostile winds,
they scour
the bare beached bones
dust to dust
yet the bones remain

imagination scurries
into hidden corners
changes shape and pattern,
in the icy stratosphere
consumed in fused energy
rekindles hope
fanning flames from embers
dying into grey-white ash.

EXPERIMENT IN RHYME

About damaged men who shrink into the quiet
at the mercy of a madwoman whose kiss
made them drunk with love fermenting a riot
in the cells that took a miss-measure of the abyss
where they lie, stabbed by the branches of dead trees
trees that will not spout green shade in a june
summer or host tangled vines of sweet peas
butterflying on the lower trunks before they prune
the leggy stems And case them in crystal
vases which shoot electric sparks above the bar
where scant clad girls belly up and hold a pistol
grip on glasses filled with amber and listen to the guitar,
plucked notes twanging dissonance, while they brood
on love among the disillusioned and how it will
conclude.

DEATH OF CAMELOT

Look into dead eyes
the last empire
of the sixties
went up
in flames
the heart
gutted,
beams smoldered
leaving ashes
blowing
in the bitter winds
keening a dirge
around
ruined temples,
soon the rains
will blow in
over uncharted
mountains
to extinguish
the last embers
a hollow volcano
empty of fire
and rumble
will stand
alone
when the night
has vanished.

Other poems by Maire Liberace
Walking on Water

This is a collection of poems celebrating Ireland, especially North Antrim. Maire has grown up with a love and regard for its history, its legends, literature and poetry. All have been embedded in the marrow of her bones and this is reflected in a deep love for the country she grew up in. And it is of these places and its people that she mainly writes. Especially Ballycastle and its environs. The people, the landscapes and, in particular, the sea always have been and still are the sources of her inspiration. Among these, Murlough Bay remains the place of her dreams and fondest memories. Many of her poems are imbued with a deep and original reflectiveness which seems to emerge from the landscape that inspired them.

Clachan Publishing

http://www.clachan-publishing.co.uk/

Other poems, ballads and songs by Clachan

Songs of the Glens of Antrim by Moiré O'Neill
These Songs of the Glens of Antrim were written by a Glenswoman in the dialect of the Glens, and chiefly for the pleasure of other Glens-people.

Away with Words - by Michael Sands
A book of poems of family, home, place and music in North Antrim.
"What a joy it has been to have discovered this marvellous collection. It represents a bright shaft of welcome sunlight in a wearying world. It is full of joy, hope, intellect and a deep understanding of who we are and the unquestioned importance of hearth, home and music." - *Mickey MacConnell, - songwriter and journalist.*

A Moment's Notice by Michael Sands
"This collection, Michael's second, is rooted in his environment: family, society, music, the natural world outside his window. Michael's poetry at times sparkles with wit and clever rhymes, and at others it is earnest in its tenderness and humanity. Underlying the verse is an encompassing love for his world and its people – turn the page, and step inside." - *Jason O'Rourke – writer and musician.*

One Man's Poison by Sarah Fox
An extraordinary collection of poems wrought through pain that leads to hope and love by a young woman who has used her experience of illness to find a distinctive voice and wisdom beyond her years.